METAVERSE

The New Digital Revolution. A Beginner's Guide to Investing in the Digital Arts of the Future, Nft, Blockchain Gaming and Cryptocurrency

© Copyright 2022 by **Jeff H. Bolton**

Table of Contents

Introduction

The connections between the financial, virtual and physical worlds have become increasingly strong. The devices we use to manage our lives allow us to access almost anything we want with a few simple steps. The crypto ecosystem works the same way. NFTs, blockchain games, and crypto payments are no longer limited to cryptocurrency geeks. They are all now readily available as part of a developing Metaverse.

The Metaverse is the concept of a persistent, online 3D universe that combines several different virtual spaces. You can see it as a future evolution of the Internet. This environment will allow users to work, meet, play, and socialize together in these 3D spaces.

The Metaverse doesn't quite exist yet, but some platforms contain some elements that come very close to this concept. Video games currently offer the closest Metaverse experience to this idea. Developers have pushed their limits with respect to what can be considered a game by organizing in-game events and creating virtual economies within them.

While not essential in this regard, cryptocurrencies can be perfect for a Metaverse. They allow you to create a digital economy with different types of utility tokens and virtual collectibles (NFTs). The Metaverse would also benefit from the use of wallets such as Trust Wallet and MetaMask. In addition, blockchain technology can provide transparent and reliable governance systems.

Metaverse-style applications already exist on the blockchain, offering people real income. Axie Infinity is a play-to-earn game that many users use to supplement their income. SecondLive and Decentraland are other examples of how to successfully blend the blockchain world and virtual reality apps.

When we look to the future, the big tech giants are looking to lead the way. However, the decentralized aspects of the blockchain industry are also providing opportunities for smaller players to participate in the development of the Metaverse.

Chapter 1: What is the Metaverse

Metaverse Definition

The Metaverse is a concept of online, 3D and virtual space that connects users together, in all aspects of their lives. This concept would lead to the linking of multiple platforms together, just as nowadays the Internet, through a single browser, allows access to multiple websites.

In essence, the concept of Metaverse is understood here as a massive infrastructure composed of virtual worlds interconnected to each other and accessible through a common interface, the browser, which incorporates both 2D and 3D elements in a kind of immersive Internet. Thus, there is no single entity called the Metaverse, rather there are multiple entities that reinforce each other through virtualization and 3D web tools that will be incorporated into our environment and become part of our lives.

The concept was developed in the science fiction novel Snow Crash by Neal Stephenson. However, although the idea of a Metaverse was only fiction in the past, it now looks like it could become a reality in the future.

The Metaverse will take advantage of augmented reality, where each user will be able to control a character or avatar. For example, you could attend a mixed reality meeting using an Oculus VR visor in your virtual office, finish work and relax with a blockchain-based game, and then manage your cryptocurrency wallet and finances, all within the Metaverse.

What distinguishes the Metaverse from the current mobile internet is mainly the dimension that we could call of co-presence, that is, the ability to feel your presence together with that of others within the same digital space. A sort of digital sensory space with three-dimensional depth, different from the flattened 2D digital space in which current technologies and platforms move. In this 3D digital space users can move freely to experience and explore it, in a way that is more natural and akin to our physical experience.

You can already see some aspects of the Metaverse in existing virtual game worlds. Games like Second Life and Fortnite, or social tools in the work world like Gather.town, bring together multiple elements of our lives in online worlds. While these applications are not the Metaverse, they come very close. The Metaverse, at present, does not yet exist.

In addition to supporting gaming or social media, the Metaverse will combine economies, digital identity, decentralized governance, and other applications. Even today, user creation combined with ownership of valuables and money are helping to develop a unique Metaverse. All of these capabilities give the blockchain great potential to power this future technology.

What the Metaverse is for

A recent article in the Wall Street Journal points to the idea that many big tech companies believe the metaverse could be the new digital revolution, after the smartphone revolution.

It could enable a new economy and have a major social impact.

Here are some applications

- Video conferencing, shared work. Facebook already has a product.
- Education, virtual guided tours of monuments.
- Immersive and experiential shopping: we will be able to better see if a dress fits us, on eCommerce.
- Purchase of houses at a distance (already in the U.S. there are virtual reality services for buying and selling real estate).
- Tourism at a distance
- Parties, virtual ceremonies
- Virtual pets
- Sports in virtual reality

Facebook and Virtual Reality: Horizon Workrooms

Facebook has recently introduced its new virtual reality application, called Horizon Workrooms, created to be used through Oculus Quest 2 VR viewers.

The challenge proposed by the colossus of Mark Zuckerberg, founder and CEO of Facebook, is to allow users from all over the world to confront each other, work, have meetings all together, within a virtual office.

Within the Oculus blog of the same name, found on Facebook, the social network has declared that Horizon Workrooms represents the future of work. The desktop application, which will be made available to both Windows users and Mac owners made by Apple, promises an excellent degree of interactivity and engagement, at levels never seen before. For example, the company said that during meetings, users will be able to physically move their desks, work computers and other materials into the virtual environment.

Horizon Workrooms will allow people to take notes and memos while meetings are taking place; it will be possible to move various files within virtual reality, sharing documents, photos, videos and presentations on others' screens. Facebook's goal, of course, is not to create a new advanced video conferencing platform, nor to aim to compete directly with other big players in the sector. According to spokesmen, in fact, the application aims to create a new way of working online. Horizon Workrooms was created to revolutionize virtual work meetings, making them much more similar to reality. One of the most interesting features is the presence of customized avatars that reflect the user himself.

In addition, the Facebook application promises extremely advanced tools such as a new spatial sound technology, which adjusts the audio and voice of your colleagues to be realistic depending on their position in the virtual room.

Facebook has thought and designed Horizon Workrooms in a versatile and comprehensive way: the application, for example, does not exclude all people who do not have access to virtual reality. Horizon Workrooms allows one or more users, without a virtual reality visor, to attend the digital meeting anyway, simply by means of a classic videoconference.

Metaverse Examples

While there is no single Metaverse yet, we have many platforms and projects that come close to this idea. Typically, these incorporate NFTs and other elements of blockchain technology. Let's look at three examples:

SecondLive

SecondLive is a 3D virtual environment where users control avatars to socialize, learn, and do business. The project also has an NFT marketplace to exchange collectibles. In September 2020, SecondLive hosted Binance Smart Chain's Harvest Festival to mark its first anniversary. The virtual expo showcased several projects from the BSC ecosystem for users to interact with and explore.

Axie Infinity

Axie Infinity is a game that offers players in developing countries the opportunity to earn a steady income. By purchasing or receiving as a gift three creatures known as Axies, a player can begin farming the SLP (Smooth Love Potion) token. By selling this token on the open market, someone could earn around $200 to $1000 (USD), depending on play time and market price.

While Axie Infinity does not provide a custom 3D character or avatar, it does offer users the opportunity for a job similar to those that might be in a Metaverse. You may have already heard the famous story of many people in the Philippines using this game as an alternative to a full-time job or government benefits.

Decentraland

Decentraland is an online digital world that combines social elements with cryptocurrencies, NFT and virtual real estate. In addition, players take an active role in the governance of the platform. As in other blockchain-based games, NFTs are used to represent collectibles. NFTs are also used for LAND, the 16 x16 meter plots of land, which users can purchase in the game using cryptocurrency named MANA. The combination of all these elements creates a complex crypto-economy.

Possible applications of the Metaverse

Here are some areas of activity, some of which are already present in Virtual Worlds.

Entertainment, gaming

One of the first and most obvious fields of application of virtuality, in all its degrees of separation from reality. The most interesting aspect will be the emergence of original gameplay within the Metaverse, using the internal resources of the world in which they take place, or the creation of virtual native shows capable of gathering an audience that compares Woodstock to a village festival.

Body and Fashion

Avatars are our representatives and therefore express not only our will, but also our desires. The body of the avatar is at the same time subject and object of desire, therefore beauty, aesthetics, fashion, the whole world of self-care and well-being have in the Metaverse and in virtual worlds a wide playing field.

Training and education

Communities of practices, laboratories, simulators. The Metaverso is the ideal place to live experiences with a strong emotional impact, but also educational. From Team Building to medical, from sailing schools to university classrooms, the virtual allows you to have memorable experiences as much as, and sometimes more than, the real thing.

Art, Theatre, Architecture and Design

The Metaverse itself is the work of creatives. The fortune of virtual worlds is the adherence of creatives to the platform, and in so doing, contributing to the construction of things, environments, objects that will make the Metaverse liveable. Without a doubt, virtual native activities are essentially creative.

Social sciences, marketing, communication

A characteristic of virtual social worlds is, so to speak, the very fast cultural metabolism that virtual world societies have. To simulate the effectiveness of a point of sale or a marketing campaign, to verify the interest of the public in a product, to create a contest or to design a hybrid real/virtual creative staff: the Metaverse allows to have answers and verifications as and better than any survey, it allows to create a prototype not only of an object, but to make a social prototype and to test it on the product.

The virtual city, geolocation

The virtual city and the real city, the map and the territory can overlap until they match, or, on the contrary, become an extension of each other. Geolocation and the combination of real and virtual are among the most promising areas.

Synthetic tourism

Synthtravel: virtual travel is not "fake travel", it is one more tool to build an opinion and experience an offer, as well as to know who will welcome us when we take the plane.

Virtual office and smart working

The evolution of identity technologies, Agile working, call conferences. All technologies and solutions for communication and work that we know well and that find in virtuality the most effective synthesis, and the big players of this market are already offering to the interest of the public and companies scenarios and products. If ever there is a booster for the Metaverse, it will once again be office automation that will pave the way, as with the web.

Virtual Real estate

Probably the first and most profitable of the virtual worlds activities have been real estate. Anshe Chung was the first virtual real estate developer in Second Life to capitalize millions of dollars in brokerage and arbitrage of virtual land.

Chapter 2: How to create a New Identity on Metaverse

Sometimes there is a strange relationship between us and our online avatars. Creating an avatar seems like a simple task, but there is actually a lot of thought that goes into it. Even if you're not thinking through every decision, the choices you make reflect your motivations for creating that avatar.

While the idea of an avatar was a bit of an odd concept when books like Snow Crash were first published, they have become incredibly commonplace in recent years. Even people who are less tech savvy will have a vague idea of what an online avatar is.

However, the types of relationships we have with these things we make to represent ourselves can vary greatly. Some people choose to remain completely private and have an avatar that looks nothing like them. They don't even want to try to recreate themselves with digital tools. Others will make an idealized version of themselves, while others will try to make the most realistic version possible.

It's amazing how virtual reality, which once seemed like something far away, has now become such a popular concept, so much so that you can now have the opportunity to create an avatar for games that use this technology. One of these is VRChat, a free virtual reality video game where players can have the opportunity to create their own character and use it to connect with other players within the game. One of the features that VRChat presents is the ability to assign an avatar to your character.

For this, a tool known as Ready Player Me (obvious reference to the movie and book Ready Player One) has been made available, a free avatar creator developed by Wolf3D that has added support for the VRChat social network where the only thing you'll need is a photograph of your face. When you experiment with using the Ready Player Me avatar creator, you will notice how easy this tool is. Once you have the result, you can have the option to import it into VRChat and select it from the game menu.

For years now, VRChat's open "avatar" system has offered users the opportunity to import their favorite character models. However, this was only possible if the person had enough experience and knowledge in development, excluding people inexperienced on the subject. Now, through this tool, anyone can create their own virtual reality avatar in a few quick steps.

Create your own avatar for VRChat with Ready Player Me

The steps you will need to follow to create your virtual reality avatar with Ready Player Me for VRChat are as follows:

- Go to the Ready Player Me for VRChat website.
- Once the page loads, click on the Create your own avatar option. This will bring up the avatar creator.
- You will then need to choose the body type of your avatar.
- Once that's done, you'll move on to the next step of the process where you can choose a photo of your face that you've already stored on your phone or PC. You can also continue the process without one to create your avatar from scratch and have the opportunity to customize different elements such as hair, eyes, clothes, among others.

Regardless of the option you chose after finishing, the next thing you'll do is click on the Import to VRChat option. This will ask you to log in to your account to give access to the Wolf3D application. You'll have to wait a few minutes for the created avatar to sync with VRChat and that's it.

Best Avatar Creation sites for Profile Pictures

You don't have to be an artist to make any of these. There are many free sites that allow you to create awesome avatars that you can customize, download and use. So whether it's Steam or some forums, here are some of the easiest ways to create an awesome avatar profile picture.

1. Avataaars Generator

The principles and standards of web design change over time. An avatar today needs to look like it belongs on the web. Since emoji is an accepted look today, this site helps you create an emoji-like avatar.

Choose hair or headgear, accessories, clothes, eyes, eyebrows, mouth and skin color. Have fun with them to create an avatar that looks like you (or the one you want to show to people online). Once you're done, download it to your hard drive.

Avataaars Generator is completely free. You can download your avatar as a PNG file or as an SVG vector graphic. You can view it as HTML or React code.

2. Face.com

Avataaars Generator is gorgeous and easy, but the things you can customize are minimal. Face.co gives you choice in every aspect of how you build your online profile avatar.

You can customize your mouth, nose, ears, eyes, eyebrows and hair. Color variations are available for your iris, hair and skin. And you can also change your clothes and add a nice background image.

To use it, connect to the service's website and choose whether to generate a male or female avatar by clicking on the displayed figures. Wait a few moments for the service's editor to load and then use the tabs at the top right to finish if you want to customize the face, eyes, hair, facial and background, the options and additional tabs below to make your choices and the palettes at the bottom left to customize the colors of what you select.

On the left side of the window you can preview your creation. The buttons below allow you to change the height and orientation of the avatar, the zoom and the tilt.

When you have created an avatar to your liking, click on the download button at the bottom right to download it immediately to your computer in SVG or PNG format (you can choose from the menu that opens). Alternatively, you can share it on Facebook or other social networks by clicking on the share button at the bottom.

You can also set your creation straight as an avatar on Gravatar by clicking on the appropriate button at the bottom of the screen. If you are not satisfied with the avatar you created and want to start over, click on the reset button and then on the ok button, while if you want to generate an avatar randomly, click on the random button.

3. 8Bit Icon

Retro 8-bit pixel art is back in a big way. Nostalgic memories of old school games and animations are popular all over the web. And, of course, that includes when it comes to creating your own avatar.

8BitIcon is very similar to Face.co, only with pixel art. Choose a background, face, clothes, mouth, hair and eyes. And even your gender.

Unusually, 8BitIcon now positions itself as a way to create avatars that are also non-fungible tokens (NFT). To request yours, you have to pay in the cryptocurrency Ethereum. Or you can simply right-click on the image and download a free PNG file via your browser.

There's not a huge variety of options on 8BitIcon, but it's pretty good. And the whole NFT angle might be a compelling reason to use it.

4. Powerpuff yourself

Cartoon Network has created a way to create an avatar from one of its most popular cartoons: the Powerpuff Girls. So go ahead and "Powerpuff Yourself."

First select your skin color, eyes, mouth, hair, beard (optional) in the Self-section . Then, go to Gear to select your clothing, glasses, an item in your hand and a companion like a dog or an object like a soccer ball. Once you are done, Powerpuff Yourself will try to create an interesting background for the avatar.

What follows is a questionnaire to determine your personality. Answer a short quiz and the app will create a wallpaper accordingly. You can download or share it as a static, animated or blank background. Beautiful, isn't it?

5. South Park Avatar

Did you know that South Park was among the first viral videos ever? So it's no surprise that the series and its creators are embracing the Internet. All episodes are available for free online and they've even created an avatar creator.

You start with a blank figure wearing underwear. Almost everything is customizable in this one. Oddly enough, because this is an official avatar creator, you get many of the official South Park animations. From catchphrases as memes to "Danishes for Denmark" t-shirts, you can do whatever you want.

You can download the avatar as a high resolution image and use it anywhere you want. Feel free to create more than one and save them all as part of your account as well.

6. DoppelMe

Would you be surprised if this site was different from everything else? Well, it really isn't. You start with a nude avatar, select small pieces from a variety of looks, styles and extras, then you're done.

Unfortunately, you only have access to all the options when you sign up for the site. But once you sign up, there are plenty of unique options, except for a nice pose.

7. Avachara

Avachara allows you to create your own anime-style avatar. In addition to skin tone and gender, you can choose from a selection of face shapes, eyes, nose, mouth, eyebrows, and hair.

You can choose from a wide range of clothes that includes everything except footwear. Choose from basic clothes and more unusual items like a construction helmet and a Santa suit. If you want to add extra items, you have a good number to choose from. There are items like guitars and swords, as well as pets, glasses and flag icons. Finally, you can choose a pattern or a background color.

When you're done, you can download your avatar as a PNG or JPEG file, in two different sizes: one full-length and the other showing only the head and shoulders.

8. Ready Player Me

With Ready Player Me, you can build your own 3D avatar. If you wish, you can upload a photo and let the site automatically create an awesome avatar for you. Or you can manually choose the bits you want to create yourself. Either way, you can choose a full-body avatar or just a head and shoulders.

As you create your avatar, you can click and drag to rotate it. Ready Player Me doesn't offer a way to change your avatar's facial features, other than eyebrows. What you can do, though, is change facial hair, hairstyle, and hair color. You can also add makeup, glasses, hats, clothes, masks and tattoos.

Once you've finished your design, you have to wait for the site to render your avatar. These avatars are designed for 3D and VR apps, so in addition to a flat PNG image, you can also download your avatar in a 3D file format.

9. Avatar Pho.to

Go to the Avatar Pho.to website and select your favorite effect from the many available, categorized. On the next page, choose, according to your needs, whether to upload the photo to be used for the avatar from the computer, by clicking on the button from the computer, or from the Internet, by clicking on the URL button or the one from Facebook.

Wait a few moments for the photo uploading to start and finish, and then you will see your animated avatar. That's it! To download it to your computer in GIF format, right-click on it and choose the appropriate item from the menu that appears.

If you want, before downloading the avatar on your PC you can also make some customizations by cropping it, adjusting the number of shots and the speed of the animations and/or adding some custom text, all through the buttons on the left.

10. PhotoFace

It is in fact an online application that allows you to generate an animated, three-dimensional and even talking avatar from your own photo. The voice can be added either by recording it or by typing a text to be read in the form of text-to-speech. All for free and from any web browser.

The only thing you have to take into account is that in order to work you must have Flash Player installed on your PC or you must use a browser that integrates it (e.g. Chrome).

To use the service, first of all connect to its website and then choose, by clicking on the buttons at the top left, if you want to upload a photo from your computer (Upload photo), if you want to take it at the moment with the webcam (Webcam) or if you want to take it from the Web (Search). If you want, you can also choose ready-made images from those at the bottom. Then specify whether the face in the photo is a man or a woman and click Next twice in a row.

Then click on the Default photo box and in the central part of the browser window you will see the preview of your avatar. If you prefer to disguise your avatar as a celebrity, click on the Be a celebrity box at the top right of the screen and select your favorite character.

Then customize the expression of your avatar using the controls on the left and the aesthetic characteristics using the additional controls below. If you want, you can also add a background by choosing from the list at the bottom left.

To make your avatar speak you must instead click on the links you find in the Add audio section. By clicking on Pre-recorder you can load a ready-made audio file, on Type In you can type a text to be spoken by the avatar, and by clicking on Use Mic you can choose to use the microphone of your PC to make a recording at the moment.

When you're done editing, choose whether to save your avatar as an image or video by clicking on the Download Image or Download Video links at the bottom right, and then click OK. Alternatively, you can decide to share the avatar via email, Facebook, direct link or embed code by selecting the other available links

I also point out that if you want, instead of using your own image, you can create a custom three-dimensional avatar from scratch. To do so, you just need to click on the Change age & gender box, make the necessary customizations related to age, gender, weight and ethnicity and proceed in a similar way as I indicated a few lines above.

Other online resources for creating your own Avatar

- Voki.com – Internet site that allows you to generate Fully customized animated avatars (although it does not support uploading your own photos) with audio in tow

- Character Creator - Website for creating a full-length avatar, both male and female.

App to create your own Avatar

To create your own avatar from mobile use the following apps:

- FaceQ (Android/iOS) - Very popular app for what concerns avatar creation that allows you to choose face type, hair, eyes, etc. and save the final image in PNG.
- Bitmoji (Android/iOS) - This is one of the most popular apps in this category. It allows you to create avatars in the style of BitStrips, the famous app for making cartoons and comics to share on social networks.
- Avatar Maker - Profile creator (Android/iOS) - Allows you to create manga-style avatars with the ability to apply numerous customizations.
- Smartphone Avatar (Android) - Very easy-to-use application that lets you generate cute avatars using various on-screen customizations. It's not exactly ideal for faithfully reproducing yourself because of the decidedly playful style, but for those who don't have this kind of mania it's a more than recommended resource.
- Myidol - 3D Avatar Creator (iOS) - App that lets you generate three-dimensional avatars that look very realistic and highly customizable.

Chapter 3: Mixed Reality

The term mixed reality (MR) encompasses the entire spectrum of technologies ranging from augmented reality to virtual reality. Reality is called mixed reality because the real world is enhanced by virtual objects, often called holograms in augmented reality terminology. The relationship between the real and the virtual determines the region of the MR spectrum in which we find ourselves.

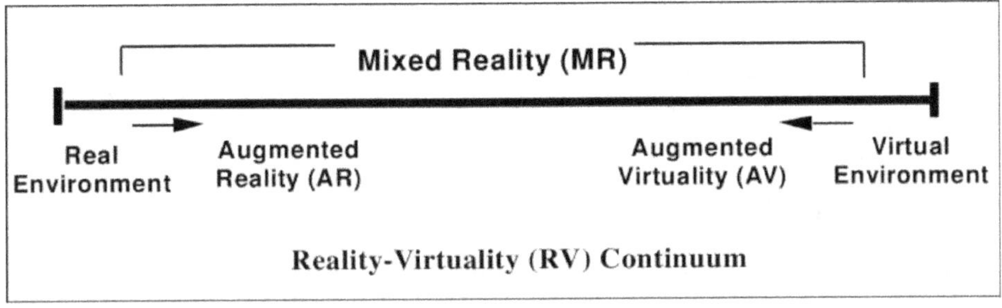

Mixed Reality evolved in recent years in Hybrid Reality, is the fusion of real and virtual environments to create new environments and scenarios. In this environment, digital and real entities exist and can interact in real time; and in this sense today its scope also includes 'augmented virtuality' that previously, at a theoretical level, had been formalized as independent.

An example of mixed/hybrid reality can be that of an operator using an immersive virtual reality application through a helmet or a visor that isolates him from the physical environment. Through this he can be monitored and guided to avoid tripping or bumping into objects in the physical environment.

For mixed reality can be used different devices such as:

- holographic devices: helmets with transparent lenses that allow you to see the surrounding environment, while virtual objects are generated through holograms.
- immersive devices: helmets with lenses that completely block the view of the real world, like VR helmets, but are equipped with cameras to monitor the real world.

Augmented Reality

If the experience of MR takes place in the real world, where a few virtual objects are superimposed on the real, we speak of augmented reality; the adjective augmented indicates precisely the addition of something that is not there, without hiding the existing, which instead is enriched with new information. The possibilities are not reduced to the mere visualization of something that was not there before; in fact, today's existing technology allows interaction with holograms, opening the doors to countless practical applications that can improve, and transform, society as we know it today.

Virtual Reality

Conversely, when the real world is completely replaced by the virtual world we speak of virtual reality, meaning that the virtual becomes the place where you are and the real reality is no longer visible, hidden behind the VR device.

The main feature of VR is immersion, that is, feeling completely captured by the virtual world, until you forget about the real one. When the experience is so similar to the real to deceive the senses, especially sight, which is our most developed sense, the user can experience the feeling that takes the name of presence.

This term means that the user feels transported into the virtual world, and assumes those behaviors that he would assume if he were in a reality equal to that recreated on the computer. An example of this is the experiment conducted by the American developer Valve, in which people, who were wearing a VR visor, were asked to move from a virtual cube on which they were and walk in a vacuum. Although they knew that in the real world there was a floor all around the virtual cube, many could not take the required step forward, feeling in some cases a strong sense of vertigo.

VR is not just passive contemplation of a computer-built world, it is also new ways of interacting with virtual objects. For people born in the last fifty or sixty years, accustomed to using a PC, or even a simple remote control to change the channel of the television, interaction with technology has always meant having to press keys or press a screen; at most, for video game enthusiasts, in addition to the key there is a stick or a trigger. However, interaction is never the mechanical, analogue interaction that everyday life teaches us. To move, we have to move our legs in a synchronized way and maintain balance to avoid ending up on the ground; by contrast, in a video game, we move by holding down a button, or tilting a stick in the direction we want to go.

One of the key ingredients of VR (but also AR) is the ability to track the head of the person immersed in the virtual world. This, in fact, is not only a possibility, but also a necessity, because it allows the user to feel transported to another world; in addition, tracking the head is essential to avoid the onset of symptoms related to nausea.

By having technology capable of tracking the head, the same technology can be applied to track the hands. One of the first commercial products for VR were tracked gloves, called DataGlove, that allowed you to manipulate virtual objects in a natural way; for example, you could grab a virtual tennis ball simply by closing your hand. Today, in what is truly a resurgence of the VR phenomenon from the heyday of the 1980s and 1990s when it seemed like VR was going to become a mainstream product, the focus has shifted from gloves to motion controllers, tracked devices that can simulate various objects, such as a gun or a racquet. In modern VR applications, motion controllers allow you to interact, in an almost natural way, with virtual objects; for example, you can operate a virtual lever by grabbing the end of it and pulling it.

Chapter 4: Augmented Reality (AR)

Augmented reality can be defined as the addition of virtual elements to the real environment, hence the term augmented.

In this definition, AR is positioned more towards the extreme of pure reality, as only a small number of virtual elements are present in the scene, which is largely dominated by the real thing (see image below).

Virtual elements, commonly referred to as holograms, can be faithful and indistinguishable copies of real objects, but also texts, sound effects and audio messages, or panels and menus that we typically see on a screen.

As we interact with reality through touch, smell, hearing, in the same way are possible interactions with holograms, depending on the particular device used: the HoloLens, for example, is able to detect hand gestures that are then translated into input used to manipulate the holograms.

The advantages of being on the mixed reality side of AR, as opposed to the opposite side, are mainly technical and usability: from a technical point of view, the fact that the ratio between the number of holograms and the number of real objects is low means that hardware performance requirements are reasonably contained; moreover, from the point of view of asset development, an AR application requires fewer models than a classic desktop, console or smartphone application.

Finally, thanks to the fact that the user has continuously the reference of the true reality, it is much less frequent the onset of negative side effects related to the detachment from reality, such as nausea and disorientation, which typically worsen the more you move from the extreme of AR to the opposite extreme of virtual reality.

The definition of augmented reality given above derives from that of mixed reality and is, therefore, very general; wanting to give a more accurate definition of AR, we can refer to that proposed in 1997 by Azuma, which summarizes the concept in question indicating three characteristics:

1. It combines virtual objects (the holograms) with the real environment.
2. Virtual objects are arranged in a manner consistent with the environment in which they are

> located; for example, a virtual painting will be aligned with the wall.
> 3. The application runs in real time and the experience is interactive.

The first point does not add anything new.

The second point introduces the concept of coherence between virtual and real, by which we mean that the relationship between virtual objects and the real environment must meet the needs of semantic coherence and functionality; for example, a virtual menu should be placed in front of the user and should not interpenetrate real objects or other holograms, thus losing solid consistency.

In order to arrange and align virtual objects in a desired manner, it is necessary for the software application to know where the user is in relation to the objects themselves and their surroundings, i.e., to be able to track the user's position and orientation.

AR applications, as per point 3, are real-time, in the sense that the application is continuously updated, processing user input and displaying graphical frames recreated taking into account the user's position at each instant. This creates the illusion that the holograms are connected to the real world. If, in addition, the experience is interactive, i.e., it is possible to perform actions that have an effect on the holograms, then the application becomes more interesting and, more importantly, potentially more useful.

Devices

This section will present the main AR devices available today.

HoloLens

Produced by Microsoft and released in 2016, HoloLens is a head-mounted display for AR, which includes an innovative tracking system based on depth sensors, RGB cameras, an integrated processor and built-in speakers.

The tracking technology is an evolution of that used by another Microsoft product, the Kinect, released in 2010 as an accessory for the Xbox 360 gaming console; to determine the position in relation to the surrounding environment, HoloLens uses two depth cameras, with which a three-dimensional reconstruction of the environment is made and simultaneously the HMD is located. This technique is a form of Simultaneous localization and mapping.

To display the holograms, the HoloLens makes use of two transparent lenses that allow you to see the real world directly, as opposed to smartphones, where reality is first captured by the camera and then reproduced on the display in an augmented way.

Interaction with holograms can take place in various ways, as the Microsoft product supports not only gesture recognition, but is also able to understand voice commands. Also included with the viewer is a small button, called a clicker, that connects, without cables, to the HoloLens via Bluetooth; the clicker can be used as an alternative to gestures or voice to provide input.

Meta

Meta is an HMD produced by the company of the same name founded in 2013 by Meron Gribetz. (Probable controversy with Facebook)

Unlike HoloLens, the Meta requires an external PC to operate, as it does not have a dedicated processing unit inside.

The first version of the Meta was successfully funded via Kickstarter2; in 2014, a version of the HMD intended for developers was released under the name Meta 1 Developer Kit.

In 2015, the company managed to raise $23 million from a venture capital firm, and in the following year, following the unveiling of version 2 of the device, Meta received another $50 million.

Version 2 of the Meta, simply called the Meta 2, offers a much higher field of view than the HoloLens, at 90°; the displays have a 2.5K resolution and 60 Hz refresh rate.

The HMD includes a front-facing RGB camera, and is capable of tracking head position. The Meta can track hands and, similar to the HoloLens, recognize certain gestures allowing interaction with holograms.

Technology

Augmenting reality in a believable and functional way requires that the entire AR system, which includes both hardware and software, meet certain specifications, such as the accuracy and robustness of the tracking system, the quality of hologram reproduction, and the speed of response to input.

The tracking system is particularly important, since the correct alignment of virtual objects with real ones depends on it; a suboptimal alignment can not only break the illusion of looking at an object actually present in the scene, but also make the application unusable. In order to correctly position the holograms, the application relies on the measurement of the position and rotation of the head (i.e., the point from which the scene is observed) that the tracking system provides to the software.

The measured values are applied to the camera of the 3D scene, which represents a hypothetical virtual observer (in this case the user), then the graphics engine performs the rendering (i.e., builds an image, the frame, by processing the given 3D models in the form of polygons and textures) of the scene and this is superimposed on reality in different ways depending on the particular technology employed.

Hand-held

By hand-held we mean a device that is held in the hand, such as a tablet or a smartphone. The very smartphone that almost every person in the world owns is an example of an AR system, as it contains all the fundamental hardware components to create an augmented reality experience:

1. Camera: smartphones, even low-end ones, are equipped with at least one rear camera.
2. Sensors (gyroscope, accelerometer): they are very common in mid- to high-end smartphones.
3. Processors and memory: the hardware of modern smartphones is comparable to PCs of a few years ago, in terms of clock frequency and number of CPU cores and amount of RAM.
4. Screen: resolutions equal to or greater than full HD3 are common in high-end devices.

A smartphone or tablet can be transformed into an AR device in the following way: the camera can be used to capture the real scene in real-time, while the sensors can be used to determine the rotation of the smartphone. The internal processor redirects the virtual objects, then combines the render produced with the frame captured by the camera; furthermore, the position of the device can be related to any references in the scene. Finally, the final composed image can be presented on screen.

Wearable

To wearable devices4 belong head-mounted displays, which can be worn like normal glasses, with the obvious advantage of keeping the hands free to perform tasks of various kinds.

One of the disadvantages of HMDs is that they are uncomfortable to wear and tiring to use for long sessions, as the devices currently on the market are not negligible in size and heavy.

Wearable devices can be of two types:

1.   Optical See-through

2.   Video See-through

Optical see-through Optical see-through is defined as a transparent or semi-transparent display that allows the user to see the real world in a natural way, even if filtered by the layers that make up the screen. The advantages (and disadvantages) of such a device are many, starting with security; in fact, even in case of malfunction, the user continues to see the real world and can react immediately and effectively in unexpected situations. From the point of view of image quality, since the user sees the real world directly, there is no loss of definition, as happens in see-through video solutions.

The main disadvantages are the limited field of view, which results in a clipped effect of the holograms, and the poor brightness and contrast, which make devices based on this technology unsuitable for use outdoors, or in a strongly lit environment.

Video see-through This technology is not only less expensive than the previous one, but it is also much easier to build devices based on it.

The image of the real world captured by a video camera is combined with the image of virtual objects and reproduced on the screen; this has a number of advantages and disadvantages.

Among the first ones, the most important is the possibility to use the device in very bright places, because it is easy to obtain a clear and sharp image of the holograms; moreover, for an optimal performance, it is possible to measure the brightness of the scene, in order to better integrate the holograms with the real environment.

On the other hand, the image definition suffers from the proximity to the display, which a few centimetres from the eyes shows the pixel structure. Above all, there is a problem due to the parallax effect that can cause disorientation in the user: in fact, due to physical limitations, the camera cannot be placed at eye level, so the captured image differs from what the eyes would naturally see. Techniques have been developed to solve this problem by aligning the images captured by the camera.

Finally, when only one screen is used for both eyes, eyestrain is significantly greater than when two separate screens are used.

Application Areas

The fields of application for AR technology are many, ranging from entertainment, medicine, architecture and the military. The more the prices of consumer products are reduced, the more affordable AR becomes and stops being something only relegated to research and military, spreading to the general public.

Gaming

In the entertainment industry, which is an industry worth hundreds of billions, AR applications are gradually catching on, especially in gaming, with a focus on smartphones.

Although today's smartphones have an enviable computational power, if compared to the first cell phones or even to the first smartphone models, and it is possible to find graphically advanced gaming applications, such as Asphalt 9 Legends and Modern Combat 5: Blackout, the particular nature of AR applications, which requires to add (and therefore process) only a limited number of virtual objects to the real background, is extremely convenient, if only from the point of view of battery consumption, not to mention the lower development costs compared to classic 3D applications.

Moreover, the portability feature of smartphones, related to the fact that we feel the need to keep the smartphone always with us, favors applications in which we take advantage of open spaces. Think, for example, of the game Pokémon GO; in this case, the entire planet in which we live becomes an immense playground.

Culture and Tourism

Museums can take advantage of technologies like Augmented Reality, both as a driver to attract younger people and as a tool to improve and make more usable their cultural offerings.

For example, one way to use AR could be an application for smartphones that, framed by a work of art with the camera, provides a description, in text or audio form, of the work itself. This could help optimize museum space, freeing up many spaces that could be occupied by many works of art that often remain "hidden."

Tourism is another one of those sectors where the spread of smartphones and AR can greatly improve the experience for travellers across the globe. Augmented reality is a potentially very useful tool because it can help tourists understand where they are, it can show them places of interest and lead them to the desired place by taking the shortest route.

Think, for example, of the possibility of enhancing and making more intuitive applications such as Google Maps, replacing the classic top-down view with directions to reach a given destination, with a more intuitive first-person view of the streets, augmented with directions on where to go. Not surprisingly, Google is working on a version of Google Maps for AR.

Education

In education, augmented reality is a valuable tool that teachers and educators, who are always looking for new ways to improve school offerings, can take advantage of to make teaching not only more effective, but also more efficient.

In fact, students are much more likely to understand and memorize through direct experience and practice, for which holograms are a valid substitute.

The ability, offered by AR technology, to enrich the scene with text, sound, 3D models, images and videos, represents an additional stimulus for the student, who feels more involved during the lesson. In addition, the audio-visual cues with which he is inundated are an aid to better understand the subject matter.

The student feels more involved because of the opportunity to interact with the holograms, having an active role in the learning process.

Examples of AR include re-enactments of historical events, such as battles and sieges, where students can observe first-hand the evolution of the battle, or chemistry applications where molecules can be visualized in three dimensions.

Architecture

Architects and designers often face difficulties in communicating project ideas to clients in a clear and understandable way in order to get feedback, either positive or negative, on various aspects of the proposed project. Augmented reality can be a great help in this, allowing the client to see a 3D reconstruction of the commissioned work in advance, before it is completed.

One of the ways AR can be exploited by architects is by visualizing the designed work in three dimensions, as virtual objects superimposed on the real world.

People interested in the project in various capacities, such as clients and managers, can evaluate with their own eyes, moving in the real environment, the validity of the proposed work, in terms of functionality, aesthetics and coherence with the surrounding environment.

The usefulness of augmented reality is not only limited to the design phase of the work, but also to the phases of construction and maintenance once the work is completed. One very useful technique is the visualization of hidden structures such as electrical cables, gas and water pipes, similar to an X-ray, but in real time.

Although AR is very interesting from the architect's perspective, it has little presence in the design and implementation processes of architectural works, mainly because it lacks proper integration with other tools, such as CAD5 software, and processes specific to architecture.

Finally, augmented reality can also play an important role in the preservation of architectural heritage; an example in this sense is the CityViewAR application developed, following the Christchurch earthquake, by the University of Canterbury. It has a dual function: to help, on the one hand, engineers visualize the buildings destroyed by the earthquake, while on the other it serves as a historical memory, reminding us of the destructive force of nature.

Military

In the military, Augmented Reality can not only be a training tool, but also a weapon to be used to one's advantage on the battlefield.

When used for the training of soldiers, we talk about Battlefield Augmented Reality System (BARS): on the real training field are scattered the various war elements in order to reconstruct a realistic war scenario. One of the main advantages is certainly economic: the use of virtual objects has a lower cost than deploying the arsenal and military means. But the real advantage lies in the possibility of reconstructing increasingly unique war scenarios in which law enforcement agencies today find themselves facing very different and complex operations.

Different is the context of the use of AR technology during real clashes, as the malfunction of the devices used on the war field can cause the injury of a soldier and the failure of the mission. One possible use of AR in this context are smart glasses that provide the soldier with additional information about mission objectives, status of comrades, and possible impending threats.

Unlike other areas, the requirements for devices used in the military are very high, due to the above, both in terms of computational power and in terms of robustness and accuracy of the tracking system.

Medicine

In the medical field, Augmented Reality has many applications, both in the operating room of a hospital, and in the bedroom or gym where a patient does rehabilitation following surgery.

An example of the use of AR to aid recovery from injury is motor rehabilitation: the patient is shown in a clear and intuitive way how to perform a given exercise or movement, so he is able to understand more easily how to perform the exercise and improves in a much more effective way.

In the operating room, AR can be a very useful support tool for surgeons and nurses: nurses are helped in locating veins or locating instruments more easily, while the surgeon can view the patient's data directly superimposed on the patient, freeing up space from monitors that can be an obstacle during surgery.

Remote health care and telemedicine are becoming more and more common, i.e. the possibility, on the part of the doctor, to assist and examine a patient remotely, via the Internet and, in fact, AR technology. The advantages are many, from the reduced economic cost both for the patient, who no longer needs to physically go to the doctor, and is not forced to wait for his turn in the clinic or doctor's office, and for the doctor, who can optimize the time of the visit.

Chapter 5: Virtual Reality

History of Virtual Reality

Already in the middle of the last century, some visionaries were talking about tools capable of simulating reality and reconstructing photo-realistic situations by computer. It was futurists of the calibre of Ivan Sutherland, Turing Prize in 1988, who created tools that, today, we could define the ancestors of virtual reality displays.

Many high-tech companies have invested billions of dollars and worked hard on virtual reality since the early 2000s. The devices have made great strides and, in recent years, have reached the homes of many curious consumers. But the possibility that virtual reality could enter our daily lives was dismissed by most people. Until the outbreak of the pandemic, interest in these technologies seemed to wane more and more, abandoned even by giants like Microsoft and Sony. In an effort to improve the user experience, virtual reality has so far proven to be little more than a niche pastime for tech enthusiasts and hobbyists. Few have been willing to spend thousands of euros to use a VR visor or tool, often bulky and inevitably connected to powerful computers.

In 2020, the turning point: the unexpected emergency situation dictated by the pandemic has radically altered every market, changing the rules of the game. The inability to leave the house and the need to stay in touch with colleagues, associates and customers made work digital. The more people worked and lived digitally, the more sales of VR viewers increased. Overall, there was an exponential increase in virtual reality hardware sales in 2020. According to research firm IDC, one of the most purchased and popular products in 2020 was the Oculus Quest 2 visor, made by Facebook.

Virtual Reality

Virtual Reality is at the opposite end of the Mixed Reality continuum from AR, as the user is completely immersed in the virtual world.

Devices

This section provides a brief review of the main VR devices on the market.

Oculus Rift CV1

After having produced two models aimed at software developers, called DK1 and DK2 (Developer Kit), Oculus releases the first version intended for the consumer market of the Oculus Rift.

Technical features The viewer uses a dual display system, with 1200×1080 pixel resolution, optical tracking system and stereo speakers.

The displays, updated to a frequency of 90 Hz, are AMOLED type, a variant of OLED technology commonly used in the production of small displays, such as those found in smartphones. The choice of OLED technology, compared to the less expensive LCD technology, is justified by the much lower response speed of OLED, which allows, through a technique called low persistence or strobing, to reduce motion blur due to the persistence of the image on the retina.

Due to the presence of two separate displays, the distance between the displays can be adjusted through a mechanical system.

Tracking System. The tracking system, called Constellation Tracking System, is optical and uses two sensors that can detect the position of the infrared LEDs covering the viewer. From these values, the tracking system determines the position and rotation of the viewer, in relation to the sensor. This is an example of an outside-in tracking system, where the sensors are external.

Oculus Rift S

In 2019, Oculus will release a new version of the Rift on the market, called Rift S. Unlike the previous version, the new visor has a single LCD screen with 2560×1440 pixel resolution and refresh-rate of 80 Hz.

In addition to the new display, Rift S also boasts a new inside-out tracking system, called Oculus Insight. Using five cameras placed on the viewer, Rift S is able to track its position and rotation in relation to the surrounding environment, it is also able to track the infrared LEDs of the controllers.

Oculus Quest

Since 2016, Oculus has announced interest in standalone devices, with the stated goal of entering directly into the mobile end of the VR market. In 2018, the Oculus Go visor is first released, followed in 2019 by the Oculus Quest.

Specifications Based on the Qualcomm Snapdragon 835 chip, the Oculus Quest is a standalone device that offers a six-degree-of-freedom tracking system (position and rotation), motion controller, OLED display with 1440×1600 resolution and 72 Hz refresh rate.

HTC Vive

The HTC Vive is the result of research carried out by Valve in the field of VR, the result of collaboration between the

Taiwanese company HTC and the American developer Valve.

Technical characteristics The characteristics of the visor are largely equal to those of the Oculus Rift CV1: the visor sports a dual AMOLED screen with a resolution of 1200×1080 pixels and refresh-rate at 90 Hz, field of view of about 110 ° (measured along the diagonal). The main difference is the tracking system, called Lighthouse, which allows the device to support a 360-degree tracking mode in a volume of a few square meters, called room-scale.

Tracking system. The Lighthouse tracking system, developed by Valve, makes use of base stations that generate laser beams; photoreceptor sensors, scattered on the viewer and controllers (or, more generally, on the object to be tracked), detect their position in space, allowing to determine the position and rotation of the tracked object.

Samsung Gear VR

In 2015, Samsung released the Samsung Gear VR, produced in collaboration with Oculus, as an accessory for its line of high-end smartphones.

The Samsung Gear VR can be seen as a much more advanced version of Google Cardboard, as it is a container in which you can place your Samsung smartphone, which will act as a display and processing unit.

Application Areas

Entertainment and culture

In recent years, thanks mainly to the new wave of commercial visors started by Oculus Rift, interest in virtual reality has been rekindled in the general public, particularly in gaming and more generally in entertainment. In addition, other activities and areas that are by nature more education-oriented, have opened up to the novelty of VR to try to attract the younger audience, usually more attentive to technological innovations; thus we can find virtual museums and theme parks, interactive theatrical performances and more.

The main driver that unites these new experiences is the sense of immersion and involvement of the public, which is no longer a passive part, but can have, if desired, an active role. The direct interaction that new virtual and augmented reality technologies allow becomes a means to communicate information in new and interesting ways.

Think, for example, of a museum that exhibits computer reconstructions of tools and machinery from the past; by wearing VR visors, the public can observe the 3D reconstruction from different angles, as if they had the original object in front of them; moreover, since it is a 3D model, it is possible to allow the public to interact with the reproduced tool or machinery, increasing on one hand the involvement, and on the other hand the learning aspect.

Examples similar to that of the machinery reproduced in 3D are the computer reconstructions of architectural elements, or even entire historic and ancient buildings, no longer existing, as destroyed by time or natural or man-made disasters. Through VR, it becomes possible to bring to life what no longer exists, and admire it with your own eyes in a more natural way than, for example, watching a reproduction on a television. In addition, thanks to the tracking system of modern VR viewers, you can move freely in a space to observe the reconstruction from different points of view.

As for gaming, the adoption of VR technology has paved the way for new genres and forms of interaction, in which the player is no longer sitting in an almost fixed position pressing the buttons of a traditional controller, but must stand and move around the game area, performing game actions in a more natural and intuitive way. One of the main benefits of this new approach to game interaction is related to physical health; by requiring the player to move, it stimulates and encourages physical activity, with positive repercussions on health.

The genres that benefit most from VR are those in which the player is inside a vehicle (as in driving games), an aircraft (as in flight simulators) or even in a fantasy car (as a Mech can be), as the sense of presence is very strong, and, above all, the negative symptoms of nausea tend to occur more rarely when the user has a solid reference (for example, the car dashboard) in his field of vision.

Other genres that are particularly well-suited for VR are those in which the player has a first-person perspective and can move naturally.

Since traditional video games are designed assuming that the player's avatar can travel great distances, the integration of virtual reality is not always immediate;

on the contrary, in many cases it is not possible to support a VR device at all, unless the game mechanics, especially those related to movement, are heavily rethought and adapted to VR.

The most used methods of locomotion today are listed here:

1. Classic movement via analogy stick: simple to implement, but should be avoided because it induces nausea.
2. Natural movement: the player physically moves around the game area. The only, and big, flaw is that the playing area is limited by the space the user has available, and by other impediments, such as cables.
3. Teleportation: the player indicates, for example via pointer on the motion controller, the point where he wants to move, then gives the command via the appropriate button. Good system to prevent nausea, but not always suitable for the type of game (think of a competitive game where participants shoot each other; teleportation would make it difficult to follow the target).
4. Portals: similar to teleportation, with the difference that the user creates a pair of portals, one of them

near where he is, and the other where he wants to go; the player enters the first one by physically moving, and finds himself outside the second one.

5. ArmSwinger: this locomotion method allows to move for long distances, while trying not to induce nausea. The player must swing his arms as if he were walking or running, but remaining physically still in place, while the avatar moves in proportion to the frequency of swinging.

Education

Living in a technological society, younger generations are familiar with the use of all forms of technology, growing up, from childhood, in contact with more or less advanced technological devices. Unlike adults, who tend to be more timid in the face of technology, young people show much less hesitation in trying out the latest innovations they hear about through advertising or word of mouth. In recent years, schools, in all its different levels from kindergarten to university, have begun to include VR and AR in their teaching processes in order to improve educational offerings.

Uses of mixed reality technologies include virtual labs, where students can interact not only with the (virtual) subject matter of the lab, but also with each other, in new and exciting ways.

An example might be a chemistry lab, where students can observe, reconstructed in three dimensions, molecules and types of bonds between atoms, from a vantage point that makes understanding the object under investigation much more intuitive.

Another example of integrating VR into education is the ability to observe the sun and planets, as well as other celestial bodies and even galaxies, in 3D, to understand, for example, how the motions of revolution and rotation of planets occur.

Architecture

When buying a house, redoing the kitchen or the bathroom, or more generally when renovating a house, it is becoming increasingly common for the client to have the opportunity to see in advance the final result of the work, faithfully reconstructed in 3D, sometimes even in immersive mode, i.e. using a Virtual Reality helmet.

This practice, called architectural visualization, allows not only the client to evaluate the result, but also the architect to verify the validity of his project. In addition, since virtual reconstruction is much less expensive and time-consuming, it is possible to make changes, even frequent ones, to the original project; by evaluating different factors and aspects of the project before the actual construction, design errors are greatly reduced.

Visiting virtually what is to be built allows, finally, to evaluate at first hand dimensions and spaces, which would be, otherwise, difficult to estimate from a technical drawing for a common person.

Another area where the ability to observe the final product before it is actually created can be extremely useful is in the construction of large buildings and skyscrapers. For example, doing a simulation of the construction can help optimize the construction process, as well as prevent any critical issues before they arise, thus reducing the time it takes to create the building.

Production and marketing

In the manufacturing phase of a product, processes based on new technologies such as virtual reality can replace traditional processes that are deemed more expensive, unsafe and inefficient.

For example, before a product reaches its final form, it undergoes a series of changes, evolving from its initial idea to become the product you find on the shelves of your local store. The prototyping process can be extremely costly and time-consuming, though necessary to achieve the quality standards required by the customer. In all, VR can be a very cost-effective and time-saving solution for prototyping, which is why it is gradually replacing the traditional prototyping process wherever possible.

In other cases, cost and production time are not the only determining factors in choosing the type of process to adopt, but also the safety of engineers, workers and company and/or institution personnel in general. VR, being by nature a simulated environment, eliminates many of the risks associated with the production of potentially dangerous machinery. In fact, a worker can be trained in the virtual environment before coming into contact with the actual machinery; on the other hand, during production, certain operations can be performed in the virtual environment to prevent any unforeseen complications, before being performed on the real machinery.

Browsing through the catalogue of an online store, it is often possible to see the products sold, from different angles, by scrolling through the photos made available to the consumer, whether it is an electronics store, or a clothing store. An alternative way to evaluate a product on sale, at least from an aesthetic point of view, would be possible by exploiting VR; whenever the user selects a product, a 3D model of it is automatically downloaded from the network, and the user can observe it in three dimensions through a VR visor [7], as if he/she had it in front of him/her in a physical store.

In fashion and in the garment industry in general, the visualization capability allowed by mixed reality technologies can be a very useful tool not only in the sales phase, but also in the production phase; think, for example, of the possibility for the designer to evaluate his new idea directly on a virtual model.

Military

In the military field, virtual reality is used as a tool for training; it is particularly useful for training soldiers to deal appropriately with conflict scenarios and unusual and dangerous situations, without running the risk of being seriously injured or dying.

Compared to traditional training methods, VR simulation is less expensive and does not put soldiers' safety at risk. Devices commonly used by soldiers in training sessions are head-mounted displays and data-gloves, both of which are tracked to allow interaction with virtual objects.

Typical training activities include

1. Training of medical personnel.
2. Simulation of armed conflict.
3. Flight simulation for pilots.
4. Driving simulation.

Virtual reality can help in treating symptoms caused by post-traumatic stress disorder (PTSD), a condition shared by many veterans who have suffered from traumas or particularly difficult psychological conditions on the battlefield. To teach patients how to manage their PTSD symptoms, they are subjected to situations that gradually trigger the disorder so that they can learn to control it, in an environment they perceive to be safe.

62

Chapter 6: Extended Reality (XR)

Extended reality as the word itself says is an extension of augmented reality, an improvement, an increase in functionality. To the augmented reality is added the function of artificial intelligence (ai). It is a generic term that includes augmented reality (ar), virtual reality (vr), mixed reality (mr) and everything else.

This term was coined to group all these technologies of visual interaction between real and digital.

This term, however, is not only to be understood as a simplification of previous concepts but as the discovery of a territory still largely unexplored, is the first step towards a growing contamination between these technologies and new forms and experiments of reality.

What is extended reality?

Extended reality is a term for technologies that create computer-generated environments or objects. This designation includes both the forms of XR already developed and those that will emerge in the future. The various technologies differ and are defined primarily by the relationship between the real and virtual worlds. While in augmented reality users perceive virtual objects as an extension of the real world, through the use of virtual reality users are immersed in a purely virtual world. Another important feature of the definition of extended reality is that it is an immersive technology in all its forms.

Definition

Extended Reality (XR): through immersive technology users find themselves in a virtual world or interact with a virtually augmented world. Virtual content is then perceived as extremely close to reality. The degree of immersion is closely linked to the possibility of interaction with the digital environment.

Chapter 7: Metaverse and Cryptocurrency

It is important to understand that the metaverse does not have to incorporate blockchain to exist, but to make the ecosystem more equitable and more secure for all participants, blockchain will play a key role in its development. With the metaverse, humans will evolve as a fully developed digital species.

Crypto meets Metaverse

Digital assets and cryptocurrencies seem to be the most vertical imperative in driving the emergence of a true metaverse. Therefore, we hear and see NFTs everywhere.

Non-fungible chips are the first step in integrating individual ownership with digital resources. A non-fungible token (NFT) is a digital item that can be created (invented), sold or purchased on an open marketplace and owned and controlled by any individual user, without the permission or support of a centralized company.

For digital items to have real and lasting value, they must exist independently of an entity that can decide to delete or disable the item at any time. What NFTs enable for the first time is a decentralized digital representation and a digital ownership layer through which deficit, uniqueness, and authenticity can be transparently managed.

Therefore, cryptography can be the necessary cornerstone for metaverses.

Why know Metaverse?

There are many cryptographic projects that are trying to develop a complete digital ecosystem based on blockchain. And because it is based on blockchain, we can participate in projects by owning their chips. One of those projects that I admire these days is Decentraland.

Decentraland is a 3D space where you can build virtual worlds, play games, explore museums full of NFT art, attend live concerts, etc. It works in a standard web browser to give you access to cryptocurrency and NFT features. You can buy and sell properties, create and sell virtual art for art galleries or build worlds. Several companies have invested in land in Decentraland and some of them may be willing to pay qualified builders for its development.

The Best Cryptocurrencies for Investing in the Metaverse

Because of what we have said, it is easy to understand how the market for cryptocurrencies related to augmented reality is rapidly expanding. Investing in Crypto Metaverse tokens could prove to be extremely productive, so let's see which are the best ones currently available on the market.

Decentraland (MANA)

The Decentraland platform with MANA tokens allows its players to purchase portions of land and use them to build/realize what they most desire (concerts, recreational spaces, land used for car driving tests). The owners of these assets are able to get real gains generated by the value imported by all users who interact with them. MANA token holders also have the right to vote on any changes that are proposed for the system, since it is based on DAO (Decentralized Autonomous Organization) technology.

Where you can buy:

https://www.etoro.com

https://www.binance.com/it

Axie Infinity (AXS)

It is a game inspired by the Pokémon universe. In fact, players can buy through AXS tokens (NFT) small animals, breed them and make them fight each other. By completing the different activities proposed by the game, users can earn, invest or sell more AXS tokens. Axie Infinity works by operating on the Ethereum blockchain, connected to Ronin (a sidechain that lowers commission costs and speeds up transactions).

Metaverse Index (MVI)

This token allows investors to invest in the world of cryptocurrencies related to the Metaverse without participating in gaming activities or virtual gaming platforms. In fact, investors can leverage the MVI token as a true ETF for the Crypto Metaverse, capturing tokens that offer various services in virtual reality environments. However, the tokens must be developed on the Ethereum blockchain and their capitalization must be greater than $50 million.

The Sandbox (SAND)

This metaverse allows its users to create, sell, and purchase unique items for use within the game experience. It is based on three main components: VoxEdit (a tool used to create the unique items or turn them into NFT SAND), the Marketplace (where artists, leveraging blockchain technology can sell their creations), Gamers (those who bring the Metaverse to life through their avatars, interacting and operating in the virtual world along with other users). SAND is an ERC-20 token based on Ethereum blockchain.

Somnium Space (CUBE)

In Somnium Space it is possible to create, buy and exchange digital worlds and NFT resources. The peculiarity of this system, based on CUBE tokens, is the fact that before making purchases or exchanges, users can experience and try the virtual worlds created. It will be possible to dine in a restaurant designed by another player, or visit an exhibition in a museum. CUBE is also based on Ethereum blockchain and is an ERC-20 utility token.

Jeff H. Bolton
METAVERSE

Chapter 8: Metaverse, Marketing, Retail and E-commerce

Although this is a technology in the development phase, with projects that are still embryonic or that have not abstractly exploited all the possibilities offered by a metaverse, the attention to this world that combines the real with the virtual is very high among marketing and communication players as well as retail and eCommerce operators.

If the metaverse acquires the power to involve people that social networks have acquired since 2008, it is clear that we are facing the new frontier of virtual interaction, capable of revolutionizing the dynamics through which to promote a product or a service, acquire and retain customers.

In the metaverse coexist and integrate with each other: virtual shops, augmented reality, NFT, streaming services, information sites, video platforms, eCommerce portals and more.

The big digital players become the "creators" of digital worlds made of patents, software, platforms, collaborations, partnerships aimed at making people live a second life (or first life) in which they can transfer a substantial part of their daily life and preserve their identity.

Among the pioneers are large fashion companies. For example, Gucci with the virtual version of the Gucci Garden open to the public within the Roblox platform. Or again, Balenciaga with its skins for Fortnite.

Of interest for industrial development is the partnership concluded between Nvidia and BMW. The objective? The creation of a "virtual original" of a factory in order to virtually plan new workflows, before applying them to the physical factory. Here's another example of the potential of real-virtual interaction systems.

Not only. In an increasingly phy-digital market, where the shopping experience must be increasingly immersive, eCommerce and retail could see with the advent of the metaverse a further boost.

The Future of Online Sales: The eCommerce Metaverse?

Imagine having a coffee with a friend of yours, sitting at a table in a coffee shop. You describe the t-shirt you would like to buy and in an instant a selection of t-shirts flashes in your peripheral vision. Digital images scroll by. Your virtual assistant, based on your preferences and thanks to artificial intelligence, fine-tunes your selection.

- And there's the t-shirt you wanted.
- With a simple gesture, you can buy the t-shirt and get (or purchase) an NFT version to dress up your holographic avatar.
- Say hello to your friend. You slip off your glasses.
- You've had coffee with a friend, purchased a t-shirt, all from the comfort of your couch at home.
- That's one of the potentials of the metaverse.

Merging the physical world with the virtual one, in order to significantly enrich the daily experiences of users.

The metaverse as a tool to offer greater access to consumers than today's material world. Or, the metaverse as a way to improve the eCommerce experience, responding to corporate and consumer needs. In other words, the speed of an online purchase, with the experience of an in-store purchase.

The eCommerce Metaverse: Instructions for Use

Since there is no single metaverse, it is not possible to provide unambiguous instructions.

Some rules of caution are, however, necessary.

Read the terms and conditions (if any) before creating your avatar and accessing the metaverse.

Do not provide sensitive and/or personal information, if you are not sure of the reliability of the platform or of the user-avatar you are interacting with.

Always remember that if you act as a consumer, there are more favorable rules.

Fashion 3.0 in the Metaverse

This evolution of the tech giants will also strongly influence fashion and sales.

Since 2020, everything has moved into the realm of ether and virtual; fashion houses will be doing shopping experiences through glasses and viewers: you can comfortably shop and try on clothes from the couch at home.

Thanks to the visor you will find yourself in the virtual world: you will be able to follow office meetings, go shopping, try on items from the new collection of your favorite designer or play.

It will be the triumph of secure shopping and customers will find virtual objects thanks to Blockchain and NFT technology and can easily access exclusive content: works of art, sports tokens collectibles.

In addition to Facebook there are Microsoft, Roblox, Epic Games, Tencent, Alibaba and ByteDance who have invested millions of dollars on the development of the project.

Mesh for Microsoft Teams will allow us to participate in video calls in avatar version even without glasses or visors: Microsoft's cloud will realize virtual reality by exploiting artificial intelligence.

Alibaba is working to prepare for the new virtual e-commerce, while ByteDance (which controls TikTok) is figuring out how to evolve video in 3D format.

Ayayi new fashion icon

Ayayi is the Chinese digital influencer so realistic that she looks real.

Lil Miquela, a virtual pop star as well as model and influencer, had appeared in 2020.

Ayayi is a "meta-human" influencer.

Influencer marketing is the main promotion tool in China for brands that want to conquer the market and the use of KOLs (Key Opinion Leaders) is one of the most efficient strategies.

The French maison Guerlain, a brand of perfumes, cosmetics and skin care products has expressed its willingness to collaborate with Ayayi.

The Metaverse, avatars and the virtual will be the future of fashion and not only.

Big giants have already understood this, but also luxury brands such as Gucci and Louis Vuitton.

The challenge will be to move from social networks to the virtual world, creating new sales channels and dressing in digital, in pixels and not in fabric.

A bet already faced by many, for example the capsule collection of Moschino for The Sims, that of the Metaverse will be a great challenge.

Chapter 9: Metaverse Investment

The metaverse is a tool that should usher in the new era. A universe where virtual reality, augmented reality and extended reality converge with the physical world. The good news for investors is that it's already possible to invest in the metaverse through a variety of investment vehicles, including stocks, ETFs, digital tokens and NFTs. Let's take a look at what's available.

Investing in Metaverse

Today, it is possible to do so by betting on stocks such as Facebook that are at the forefront of the development of this digital world, or on cryptocurrencies such as Decentraland that were the first to offer the opportunity to buy goods and services in a parallel reality.

More and more companies have decided to invest money in research and development projects in this area, as well as more and more crypto based on virtual worlds where you can use your tokens.

Let's see how we can invest in this market that will certainly explode in the future.

SHARES

The first option for investing in the metaverse is about buying the equities of companies related to this virtual reality.

Here are the 5 most relevant ones to buy and keep in your portfolio:

Facebook Metaverse: investing in a "Social" Metaverse

Meta, the new name of the Holding Company that controls Facebook, Instagram, Oculus, WhatsApp and many other tech and fin-tech start-ups.

As stated in the Facebook Connect the presentation event of Facebook's Metaverse project, the social experience will be increasingly linked to the Metaverse, augmented and virtual reality.

Meta's goal is to bring the metaverse into people's homes. In other words, Meta wants to turn the metaverse into reality.

Zuckerberg said that Meta is investing heavily, and indeed will invest more and more, to implement the hardware and software technology needed to create the metaverse.

Let's see in practice what these investments translate into.

Oculus VR

Oculus VR produces virtual reality viewers. Its flagship product is the Oculus Quest visor.

Project Cambria

Project Cambria is the new series of devices to have access to virtual reality. It promises an extra level of immersion, as it will also feature internal sensors to monitor eye and face movements. This will allow you to more effectively communicate emotions and moods while interacting with other people.

Horizon Home

Horizon Home allows the creation and customization of digital environments to share with friends and family on the metaverse. In other words, Horizon Home lets you create a metaverse for your private life.

Horizon Worlds

Horizon World allows the creation and customization of gaming environments.

Horizon Workrooms

Horizon Workrooms is a virtual reality (VR) application for remote work. Horizon Workrooms is a kind of digital office for the "business" metaverse, which you can access with an Oculus VR visor.

Horizon Venues

Horizon Venues is a virtual reality (VR) application for online events.

Spark AR

Spark AR is a tool that allows users to create their own augmented reality (AR) effects for mobile devices.

Microsoft Metaverse

As mentioned the Microsoft metaverse is very much focused on the working world. A sort of "Business" metaverse, for companies. Microsoft proposes to create a digital copy of the world, a "Digital Twin", in which are present all the data collected by the real model.

This data can then be used for endless applications. For example to remotely drive machines, trigger alarms, optimize processes, monitor reality, increase security, etc.... In a nutshell anything can be managed, automated and optimized with the right information.

To achieve this metaverse, Microsoft is creating a number of metaverse projects. Let's look at the main ones:

Microsoft Mesh e Hololens

Microsoft Mesh and Hololens enables anyone across the planet to collaborate in mixed reality environments.

Microsoft Power Platform

Microsoft Power Platform enables anyone within a company to interact with the data flowing through the environment. It allows you to create intelligent applications, dashboards and chatbots that modernize workflows.

Azure AI & Autonomous Systems

Azure AI & Autonomous Systems is based on Artificial Intelligence. It offers in-depth insights into all of a company's data.

Microsoft Project Bonsai

Microsoft Project Bonsai provides a low-code approach to machine learning and deep learning for creating intelligent autonomous systems.

Azure Synapse Analytics

Azure Synapse Analytics is a comprehensive set of data services that interact to provide historical and predictive analytics.

Azure Maps

Private indoor space maps allow you to apply location and routing services to people and things in your private environment, while keeping the data in-house.

Azure Digital Twins

Azure Digital Twins simplifies the creation of detailed and comprehensive digital models. It enables modelling of complex relationships between things and systems in the environment.

Azure IoT

Azure IoT enables the interaction between reality, virtual reality and augmented reality. Monitor and analyze anything in your physical environment transparently and securely.

Nvidia

The digital world and augmented reality need an extremely solid technological infrastructure. Nvidia, thanks to its know-how and its cutting-edge products, is perfect for the creation of these digital platforms.

For some time now the company has been working on projects related to the Metaverse, in particular with the development of Omniverse, a specific platform for this new world.

NVDA stock is already experiencing a Bull Run on the Nasdaq that has few equals in the world, with this new collaboration its bullish march could continue for a long time yet.

Roblox

An innovative video game company listed on the NYSE since March 2021, Roblox is at the forefront of building the virtual ecosystem based on the metaverse.

Already for some time some videogames allow you to interact in a virtual context, wearing 3D glasses, think of well-known games like Fortnite. However Roblox is much more: to date it is a company that has a platform where users can create their own games or create virtual events (such as the Gucci fashion show), using the digital currency of Roblox.

Basically, Roblox has already created its own virtual world based on the metaverse and with further development of this sector it will be able to bring all its expertise to bear. The stock on the Stock Exchange has reacted very well to these indiscretions and the target set by analysts exceeds $100 per share.

Shopify

Here is another company that could benefit enormously from the development of the metaverse: Shopify.

A company specializing in e-commerce, it is already investing in digital platforms capable of supporting payments (in cryptocurrency) within these virtual realities. Its expertise in payments and online shops has made this company perfect for the needs of the metaverse.

Already today a specific platform in NFT Token has been launched where to buy and sell contents related to the art world with other connected users. We are probably just at the beginning of a much larger process!

Investing in the metaverse with NFTs

As we have seen, the metaverse is a sort of digital parallel world, made of avatars, public and private digital environments. As in reality these environments must have some "basic" elements accessible to anyone, so that anyone can access the metaverse. As for social, if you are alone there is no fun. For it to be interesting, everyone must participate.

Access to the metaverse must therefore be democratic. However, not everything will be free. There will always be someone interested in having something extra. Something that others can't have, and that sets you apart from the crowd.

And that's where Non Fungible Tokens (NFT) come in.

Imagine you've created the digital home, your "meta" home, and you want to give it a special touch. A beautiful painting. You can open Paint and paint an awesome DIY digital painting. Or you can buy a "meta" painting, made by some famous artist. The choice is yours.

But be careful what your friends think when they visit your "meta" home!

Joking aside, as it happens in real life, also in the metaverse people will want something unique and not freely reproducible.

NFTs will allow you to certify that you are the only one who owns the rights to a digital asset.

A digital asset can be anything! A painting, an avatar jacket, a monster, a means of transportation, an entire house, an entire world!

Investing in the metaverse through NFTs means building NFTs to sell them or buying NFTs to resell them at a higher price.

For example, let's go back to our meta framework. Imagine you buy the NFT of the meta painting of some semi-unknown artist and after a few years this artist becomes famous. Now the NFT of your digital artwork is worth much more!

In short investing in the right NFT, now when most of the population is still unaware and therefore the demand is still low can allow you to make very interesting profits.

Of course the risk is very high.

The metaverse is still far from the masses and it's doubtful that people will ever be interested in creating a parallel digital life for themselves. And even if that happens, it's not certain that people will be interested in your NFT.

As a result, you can opt for a "less risky" solution: investing in cryptocurrencies.

Investing in the metaverse with cryptocurrencies and Ethereum

Investing in the metaverse with cryptocurrencies means investing on the layer on which NFTs are based.

To ensure "ownership" of digital assets, NFTs rely on the blockchain. The reward for those who process the blocks are cryptocurrencies. Consequently, as the metaverse, and therefore NFTs, spread, it is inevitable that the value of the cryptocurrencies underlying these assets will also increase in value.

NFTs usually rely on the blockchain technologies of:

- Bitcoin
- Ethereum
- Solana
- Polkadot
- other crypto derivatives

Invest in metaverse stocks by investing in companies working on the blockchain

Let's take it up a level further and get away from the true nature of the metaverse: investing in shares of companies that work on the blockchain. The easiest way is to invest in publicly traded companies, as you can buy shares on the markets pretty easily.

If you want to invest in "metaverse" stocks, there is a problem you have to face: you have to be able to estimate the fair value of the company's shares. That is, you have to analyze the balance sheet and establish, based on the current state and your growth estimates, a reasonable price for the shares. If the value of the stock you have estimated is greater than the current price at which the stock is trading then it will make sense to buy it. Otherwise, you will have to wait for the listing price to align with the value you have estimated.

What is the problem?

Estimating the fair value of "Metaverse" shares is virtually impossible.

Very little is currently known about the state of the technology. But even less is known about the possible gains the metaverse will bring to the companies developing it. This means that it is not possible to have an idea of the real value of these companies.

In any case, this "exercise" is critical to investing consciously in metaverse stocks.

If you don't feel ready to do this then it's probably best to leave it alone. Investing based on emotion or the presumption that you know the price will rise is one of the biggest mistakes investors make.

Fortunately, a problem can always be solved when money is involved.

In fact, recently there have been funds created, called Exchange Traded Funds (ETFs), that invest in companies that work on the blockchain. By buying shares in these funds you will automatically buy shares in the best companies that use the blockchain or work on blockchain technology.

Investing in markets linked to the metaverse

Making the metaverse possible requires more than just Facebook, Microsoft, NFTs and the blockchain. The metaverse involves a lot of sectors and markets. Here are some markets that could enjoy the growth of the metaverse, the name of some stocks of companies operating in the market. Finally, in the last column of the table you can find " the label" used by the main indices, if for example you wanted to invest in the metaverse with ETFs on related sectors.

Market	Metaverse related actions	Metaverse Related ETF Indices
Metaverso Platforms	Facebook, Microsoft	–
3D reality scanning	Matterport	Automation and Robotis
Data analysis & Cyber Security	Palantir, Alibaba	Artificial Intelligence and Big Data; Cybersecurity and Data Pravacy
Gaming and 3D Modeling	Autodesk, Electronic Arts, Tencent	Gaming Esports
Chipmakers	Nvidia, Intel	Semiconductors

Lenses and glasses	Essilorluxottica	-
Telecommunications	Huawei	Communication services

Why invest in the Metaverse?

Investors are wondering if it is worth investing in the metaverse or if we are facing a bubble that will soon explode.

After analyzing in detail everything that revolves around this ecosystem, we have found these 5 advantages that make it worthwhile to invest in the metaverse, especially with a medium and long term horizon:

- Innovative sector: we are in front of a new and still unexplored branch of Business, the growth margins are huge.
- Substantial investments: in the last few months alone, Facebook has invested over 50 million dollars in the development of the metaverse. Other financial giants are also doing the same, a clear sign of an interest that will not be exhausted in a short time.
- Profitable tokens: already now, the so-called NFT tokens are in great demand due to the excellent performance achieved on the market and the

innovations made. The metaverse will represent an additional reason to buy these digital currencies.

- Access costs: on regulated platforms it only takes $50 to start investing and create a diversified and well-structured portfolio with stocks, ETFs and cryptocurrencies linked to the metaverse.
- Cutting-edge project: investing in the metaverse means investing in the future, an aspect that stimulates the interest and imagination of investors from all over the world.

These 5 aspects alone make the opportunity to invest in this field interesting, obviously the next months will be crucial to better determine the evolution of the metaverse and its application in the real world.

Which markets are likely to go down because of the Metaverse?

Just as it will mark the success of many companies, the metaverse will also lead to the downfall of others. Many markets will be negatively impacted by the growth of the metaverse.

Think, for example, of all the business travel that was going on before the advent of 2020. That year was a watershed year in this regard. Remote meetings suddenly became the norm. Many workers who once worked in an office have started working remotely. All with no small amount of difficulty. But by now the initial resistance has been broken so there's no going back!

Smart working is here to stay, and the metaverse will make it even easier and on the agenda.

Workers will no longer have to go to the office but will be able to work from home or some other location specifically set up for the metaverse.

With fewer offices there will be fewer rush hours, fewer meals at cafeterias or restaurants, fewer vending machines to stock, fewer hours spent cleaning offices.

In short, things will change. Only time will tell.

Returning to a more concrete discussion. The sectors that will certainly be negatively impacted are all those related to travel.

If people can move freely and at very low cost in the digital world, they will inevitably move less in the real world.

The most impacted sectors will therefore be:

- tourism
- Transportation (especially airlines)
- the commercial rental market

Controversies

Since this is a completely new industry, there are still some unclear or otherwise controversial aspects surrounding the metaverse.

Here are the main criticisms made of this new digital world:

Closure to the outside world: is there really a risk of cutting the bridges with the real world to spend more and more time to the point of locking oneself in this virtual reality? An issue that troubles several interviewees.

Who will manage the metaverse?: clearly the role of Governance has yet to be debated, but it represents a crucial theme for the development of this sector.

How many metaverses will there be?: some wonder if there will be a single platform to which we will all have access or if there will be dozens and dozens of parallel metaverses.

How will security be managed: fraud, payment security, privacy management: these are all aspects that deserve a precise answer.

Obviously, being a project in its infancy, it is not easy to give specific answers to each critical issue that is raised. Only when a platform of the metaverse will be introduced in an official way then it will be possible to provide a detailed answer.

Summary

The best stocks in the metaverse to buy today

In addition to Meta (MVRS) and Microsoft Corporation (MSFT) here are what might be the best stocks in the Metaverse to invest in the near future.

Unity Software Inc. (U)

Unity Software has one of the two leading 3D video game engines, allowing designers to customize the way video game players move and interact within their games. In fact, 94 of the largest 100 game development studios use the Unity engine.

During Unity's second quarter earnings release, CEO John Riccitiello said that the 'company will support and shape the metaverse' and 'emphasize content creation, cross-platform access, narrowing the gap and reducing friction between creators and consumers.'

Unity can be a central player in helping companies create unique Metaverse presences, the equivalent of today's Web sites or social media pages.

Roblox Corp. (RBLX)

Roblox is an online entertainment platform that may be the closest thing to a social metaverse in existence today.

Roblox is essentially a video game that has 43.2 million daily active users, its own digital currency, and a wide range of unique virtual experiences, such as a live digital Lil Nas X concert in 2020.

Outside developers are constantly creating new games and content to integrate into the existing game, which serves as the foundation for the growing metaverse. The platform's 1.3 million developers are on track to collectively earn $500 million from their creations in 2021.

Amazon.com Inc. (AMZN)

For years, Amazon has focused on expanding its e-commerce platform into an 'ecosystem', integrating shopping, entertainment and cloud services for its users.

Amazon has the dominant online shopping platform and will likely look to establish a version of an 'Amazon mall in the metaverse' where shoppers can interact and purchase digital products.

In a recent post, Amazon's Vince Koh, who leads global digital commerce for the company, discussed innovations such as virtual trials, virtual pop-up stores and a virtual avatar economy as ideas that would change the retail landscape. Finally, Amazon Web Services will likely play an important role in creating and maintaining the Metaverse's infrastructure.

Autodesk Inc. (ADSK)

Approximately 70% of Autodesk's business comes from architectural, engineering, and construction (AEC) design software. Engineers and architects use the Autodesk application to virtually design 3D buildings and infrastructure projects.

Autodesk now has a suite of products designed specifically for creating animations and buildings in 3D virtual and augmented reality, a perfect solution for building the metaverse. In the second quarter, Autodesk's AEC segment revenue grew 21% to $397 million, while media and entertainment segment revenue grew 10% to $53.3 million.

It's easy to see why Autodesk is the best choice for developers creating the first metaverse.

Nvidia Corporation (NVDA)

Nvidia produces the graphics and video processing chips used in high-end computing servers, supercomputers, artificial intelligence and virtual reality applications.

Nvidia chips will play a crucial role in providing the massive amount of processing power required by the metaverse.

Nvidia is also creating its own Metaverse platform, called Nvidia Omniverse. Nvidia Omniverse is a platform used to connect 3D worlds into an integrated virtual universe. The company said Omniverse can be used for a wide range of enterprise applications, such as design collaboration and real-world architecture simulation. In addition, Nvidia says Omniverse is a useful tool for training robots.

Conclusions

The Metaverse is the fusion of augmented reality, virtual reality and social.

The two ambassadors of the metaverse in the world are Meta Platforms (Facebook) and Microsoft. However, these two players have two different conceptions of the metaverse.

The metaverse for Microsoft is much more related to business and technology applications and monitoring related to augmented reality, virtual reality and management. For Microsoft the metaverse is about creating a digital copy of reality, with which to monitor everything to have data to analyze.

Facebook's metaverse is much more like a game. Not for nothing does it come from the leading company in the world of social. In this case the idea of metaverse is related to a fantasy world where people can create avatars, interact with each other and with the world.

If you want to invest in the metaverse you could then consider investing in the shares of these two companies. Alternatively, you could invest in other companies that operate in markets somehow related to the metaverse.

These include:

- 3D reality scanning

- 3D modelling
- Data analysis & Cyber Security
- Gaming companies
- Chip manufacturers
- Lenses & Glasses
- Telecommunications

Finally, you could invest in what will be the future ingredients of the metaverse: NFTs. However, investing in the single NFT can be very risky, in the sense that the probability of buying something that has no real value is very high. Consequently, to mitigate the risk, you could invest in the infrastructure behind the NFTs. For example, you could:

- invest in cryptocurrencies
- invest in shares of companies that develop the blockchain
- invest in funds that invest in shares of companies that develop the blockchain

Chapter 10: Metaverse ETF

The Roundhill Ball Metaverse ETF (META) seeks to combine the physical and virtual worlds into a single fund. The "Metaverse" has become a popular buzzword in the financial markets, so much so that Facebook (FB) actually renamed itself Meta Platforms to reflect its new strategic direction.

In this chapter, we will discuss Metaverse investing, beginning by defining what ETFs are.

What are ETFs?

ETFs (Exchange Traded Funds) are special investment funds (or Sicavs) that are passively managed. As with all funds, when you buy an ETF is as if you were buying a basket of securities. Investing in a fund is equivalent to putting your savings together with those of other investors, the fund manager will then buy with this money the instruments in which you are going to invest. The performance of the investment will be given by the result of all the individual instruments in which the fund invests.

Advantages of ETFs

1. Cash

As listed instruments, ETFs are extremely liquid instruments. This means that it is easy to buy or sell new shares without running the risk of seeing their value fall.

2. Transparency

The high degree of investment transparency is inherent in the very nature of ETFs. It is easy to get a complete picture of the instrument from various points of view: from currency exposure to creditworthiness, from managed assets to the type of replication.

3. Versatility

Thanks to ETFs, even the small saver can access the main market indices without having to buy all the securities in the basket.

4. Security

The assets invested in ETFs are separate from those of the company which issues them and manages them, and are therefore returned even in the event of its bankruptcy.

5. Efficiency

Passive management makes investing in ETFs extremely profitable. Consider that the management cost of an ETF hardly exceeds 0.5%, while that of an active fund exceeds 2%.

6. Strategy

ETFs make it easier and more cost-effective to develop multi-asset strategies that take advantage of medium-term market growth trends, based on macroeconomic trends.

How ETFs Work

The peculiarity of ETFs is that they are funds that adopt passive strategies. This means that ETFs aim to replicate the performance of a specific index or the price of a specific asset class.

The ETF on the FTSE Mib, for example, will have the same daily result as this stock market index, just as an ETF on the price of gold will replicate the variations in the price of this market. In order to achieve this objective, the managers of an ETF purchase shares of securities of the reference indices - technically called benchmarks - in a quantity proportional to the resources available. In this way, the value of the investment will be exactly the same as that of the replicated index.

Unlike active funds, therefore, where the manager has a wide discretion in buying securities to try to generate yield, when you buy an ETF you already know in which type of product your savings will be invested: the performance will therefore not depend on the ability of the manager but on the trend of the chosen index.

Which ETFs to choose?

When selecting ETFs, you should not only look at the asset class they refer to. In fact, if you decide to invest in a single asset class, there are many different options. How do you choose between two different ETFs whose performance is linked to the same index?

Here are all the factors to consider:

- The amount of assets the fund managers, which determines its liquidity.
- The replication strategy, physical or synthetic, preferring the former where possible.
- The cost.
- The reference currency.
- The provider, i.e. the management company of the fund, giving preference to companies of proven quality.
- Premium/discount: at certain times, when there is particular demand for a product, it is

> possible to create a premium or a discount at the time of the sale of one's shares.

ETFs are extremely practical and usually inexpensive instruments. In recent years they have gained in popularity as the ability of active management to outperform the benchmark consistently - at higher costs than passive management - has been questioned.

ETFs are listed on the stock exchange and ETF units can be bought and sold at any time, just as if they were normal shares or bonds.

Metaverse ETF

It was almost a given that ETF issuers would follow the trend and launch a fund in an attempt to capture the meta universe in a single portfolio. The Roundhill Ball Metaverse ETF (META) was launched in June 2021 and replicates an index that "is composed of a hierarchically weighted combination of global listed companies that actively participate in the Metaverse."

In terms of the "layered weighting" concept, META will give more weight and ranking to companies it considers pure business, assigning lower positions to "core" and "non-core" names.

"Pure-Play" companies - A company whose primary business model and/or growth prospects are directly related to the Metaverse. For these companies, continued Metaverse growth should be critical to their future economic success.

"Core" Companies - A company with primary operations and/or prospects for growth related to the Metaverse. The economics of these companies are based on other business units, and thus they are less affected by growth in the Metaverse than pure-play companies. However, if the operations in the Metaverse, of these companies become primary in their economic performance, then, they may become pure-play companies.

"Non-core" companies – A company that has operational and/or growth prospects related to the Metaverse. Most of these companies' revenue comes from lines of business that are not directly related to the Metaverse. Over time, if these companies' operations in the Metaverse become drivers of economic performance, over time, industry growth and/or investments in specific sectors in the Metaverse may cause these companies to become "core" "companies." Based on current information, it is unlikely that specific Metaverse products from non-core companies will become the primary driver of this economic performance in the future.

According to Roundhill, the initial weight of pure business companies is two and a half times that of core companies or five times that of non-core companies, and the initial weight of core companies is twice that of non-core companies.

META Portfolio Composition

Although META tends to focus primarily on large-cap and large-cap companies, its distribution in technology and communications services is highly diversified.

No individual in the portfolio is truly overweight. Of course, there are some gaming platforms, such as Roblox. Social networking platforms, such as Facebook, will also provide gaming and communication experiences, with relatively little weight, but some impact.

Then there are the names for most of the graphics, interfaces and communication tools provided in the Metaverse. Nvidia is the largest holding in the fund, but Unity Software, Microsoft and TSMC are also in the top 10.

The fund is relatively concentrated in a total of about 40 names. Although it targets the meta universe, it is primarily a technology ETF. Surprisingly, META is not as highly correlated with traditional technology-focused funds. Its correlation coefficient with Invesco QQQ Trust (QQQ) and Technology Select Sector SPDR ETF (XLK) is between 0.75

and 0.80. The highest correlation is with First Trust Dow Jones Internet Index ETF (FDN), which is about 0.88.

It's too early to call META the ultimate success, but it looks like it's already well on its way. The investor interest is there. As consumer awareness and acceptance improves, I expect this foundation to do better.

META's total assets exceeded $400 million, a good start for this fund that has only been established for five months. However, its initial success can be considered a fluke. The ETF is off to a good start and generally growing slowly and steadily, but as of a month ago its assets are still slightly over $100 million.

An expense ratio of 0.75% is a bit high for index funds, but not entirely unusual for thematic ETFs. Can I invest now? It still has room for improvement. The trading spread is still a bit high and slightly off its net asset value. The average daily trading volume is only about $3 million USD, so there aren't many buyers and sellers. If you really want to get into the metaverse trend now, it might be acceptable, but it should improve over time.

Chapter 11: How to sell characters in CryptoBlades

CryptoBlades is a new NFT role-playing game that runs on blockchain.

In the game, players can recruit characters, fight them for EXP and level up.

Characters in CryptoBlades are NFTs that can be traded and sold in the marketplace.

Here are the steps on how to sell your CryptoBlades characters in the marketplace:

- Go to the Market tab
- Click the "NFT List" button
- Click the "Show Characters" button
- Select the character you want to sell
- Click on the "Character List" button
- Enter the selling price of your character in SKILL

After a few moments, the character will disappear from your Plaza.

Note that whatever SKILL price you enter in the input box, the game will add a 10% commission.

This means that if you enter 1 SKILL on the sale price of your character, other players will pay 1.1 SKILL to buy him on the market.

Finally, as with most activities in CryptoBlades, you will need a small amount of BNB gas when you put characters or weapons up for sale on the market.

So make sure to leave a small amount of BNB tokens on your portfolio if you want to trade!

How to value my characters

NFTs on CryptoBlade such as characters and weapons are traded freely in the marketplace.

Players are free to enter any SKILL price amount for their characters when selling them on the market.

There are no hard and fast rules or formulas for determining how much a character should cost. In fact, these prices can fluctuate greatly due to many factors.

However, you can check the current market value of characters based on their level and stats to get an idea of how much you should value your characters when you sell them.

Here are the steps on how to check the current market value of CryptoBlades characters:

- Go to the Market tab
- Click on "Browse NFTs"
- Click on "Browse Characters"

Here you'll see a list of all the characters put up for sale by other players.

This should give you an idea of how much SKILL token characters are being sold on the market based on their level and stats. You can also use the filtering and sorting features to check the prices of characters with a specific level or item.

How to sell your CryptoBlades characters

When you put your character up for sale on the market, other players will be able to see it while searching for NFT.

If you're lucky, some random player might see it and buy it instantly. However, this may not always be the case.

That's why, in addition to putting their characters on the market, most players also "promote" them on online communities like Discord or Reddit.

Here are some places where you can sell your CryptoBlades characters (or weapons):

- CryptoBlades Official Discord Server
- CryptoBlades Market Server Discord
- CryptoBlades Market Subreddit
- CryptoBlades Twitter

To promote the characters you are selling, take a screenshot of your character/weapons and post it on message boards/chats. Be sure to copy and paste the character's NFT ID as well.

If other players see your listing and are interested in buying, they can simply copy the character's NFT ID and search for it on the CryptoBlades marketplace using the "Search NFT" feature.

How to verify if your character is listed for sale

To check if your character is actually listed for sale in the Marketplace, follow these steps:

- Go to the Marketplace tab
- Click on "Search NFT"
- Click on "Show My Characters"

This will show you a list of your characters that you have listed for sale in the Marketplace.

Other players should be able to see it and purchase it if they are interested.

Currently, there are no real-time notifications telling you that your characters have already been purchased by a player.

You simply need to manually check if your SKILL balance has increased and your character has already disappeared from the list.

Chapter 12: Technologies of the Metaverse

The metaverses we will mention involve a very wide range of technologies and are the first step towards something more ambitious, able to overcome the conception of the dystopian world, completely alternative to the real one. The metaverse is destined to evolve in the coexistence of real content and virtual content capable of representing the entire continuum of reality.

To enable this vision, a digital model of the physical world is required, where immersive 3D technologies such as virtual and augmented reality can add the digital content that can create an infinite series of experiences based on the real world.

Unlike dystopian worlds, which characterize an escape from reality, the metaverse based on the real world involves the possibility of creating simulations and interactions with the reality that surrounds us, with disruptive effects even in the enterprise world, going beyond the playful and social manifestation of the first experiences that we have analyzed.

The indispensable components to enable this paradigm of the metaverse fundamentally reside in three 3D technologies, still well-known but currently far from the level of maturity that would be required to create virtual worlds with the same realism of that in which we are used to live our experiences.

Digital Twin 3D

This is a 3D technology capable of creating a digital model of an entity present in the real world, to interface it through information layers, sensors, IoT systems. A digital twin allows to acquire information in real time from the physical model to interact with it through digital systems. This is a technology that already enjoys a good diffusion in the scale of the single object / artifact, as evidenced by the cases of application in Industry 4.0, but still quite immature in urban and territorial scale, especially for the current limits at the computational level.

When Sweeney affirms that to create the contents of the metaverse will need the work of millions of people, he also refers to the fact that replicating the real world in 3D requires a colossal effort in which technique and creativity should also converge in shared protocols and positions, capable of guaranteeing an open and interoperable format to create the layers of the virtual world.

Until each big tech develops its own proprietary system, think of Google Earth or Microsoft Bing, it will not be easy to find a reference environment. As it stands, open source projects like OpenStreetMap don't have the level of implementation to warrant such a solution.

When we talk about a real-world digital twin, we often come across the term Mirrorworld, the mirror world that increasingly finds in the cloud the computational resources and technologies needed to generate and visualize the billions of polygons that realistic 3D models inevitably entail once the environments reach a certain size.

To facilitate this task, the current graphics engines allow to scale the level of detail (LoD) of geometries as a function of the distance from the point of observation and the cloud allows to exploit artificial intelligence techniques to recognize the perimeter of objects on photogrammetric surveys to accelerate the production of 3D models [for more information on AI, we recommend reading our guide to artificial intelligence that explains what it is, what it is used for and what are the application examples - ed.]

One example of a very advanced mirrorworld is Flight Simulator, which leverages a wide range of cloud technologies from Microsoft Azure and Microsoft Bing to allow virtual pilots to fly over incredibly realistic scenarios. The gaming experience developed by France's Asobo Studios will be a pilot project for enterprise applications.

AR Cloud

Otherwise known as spatial computing, this is an augmented reality technology implemented in the cloud, capable of adding informative layers to the real world. The particularity of spatial computing lies in the fact that digitally generated content is persistent, as the data is tracked against the physical environment and stored in the cloud, to be always accessible by all users involved in the metaverse.

In other words, if I create a 3D content like a teapot and thanks to an AR Cloud application I place it on a real table, it remains there even when I end a work session. The moment I activate a new session, I'll find my augmented reality teapot exactly where I left it, unless another user sharing the same project has moved it in the meantime. Easier done than said.

As of today, there are already a few AR Cloud applications within collaboration platforms that allow for both multi-presence meetings and review and shared design sessions between multiple users. The main feature of such environments is their hybrid nature, allowing for the simultaneous use of traditional, augmented reality and virtual reality tools. Some users may work in physical proximity, others connected from other locations, but all share the same virtual environment. The best-known native VR collaboration tool is currently Spatial, but immersive modules are currently being developed for the most widely used platforms globally, such as Teams, Zoom and Webex.

The limitations of cloud AR technologies lie mainly in the fact that augmented reality devices are still rather limited from a computational point of view, and at the same time insist on significant latencies when accessing computational resources in the cloud. The diffusion of fast and broadband connections such as 5G is in fact the main enabling condition for applications based on spatial computing.

Virtual Reality

Among the technologies that allow to create virtual worlds in 3D, VR is undoubtedly the one able to guarantee the highest level of immersion and presence in the digital experience. This is enough to explain its importance in the context of the creation of a metaverse. Its combination with digital twin and spatial computing allows to guarantee the whole continuum of realities, ranging from the real world to the fully virtual world, where all the intermediate states are constituted by the various levels of augmented reality.

Virtual reality is a technology that is spreading quite rapidly both at enterprise and consumer level, even if we are far from the moment in which we can actually consider it a massively diffused technology.

Oculus represents at the moment the most widespread VR ecosystem at consumer level, thanks to the commercial success of the Quest 2 visor, but the so-called killer app has not yet arrived, the application able to explode the diffusion of a certain technology. At the moment VR is widespread in all contexts, even if the most significant numbers are recorded in the gaming sector, as confirmed by the success of PlayStation VR.

In the enterprise environment, VR is widespread in the context of Industry 4.0, to carry out simulations without having to resort to the physical availability of plants and artifacts, as well as to try risky situations without endangering operators or causing a production stoppage on the lines. These are aspects that make virtual reality particularly popular for applications in training.

Chapter 13: Metaverse and Future

While we are writing these lines, it seems quite easy to imagine a metaverse in one of its many manifestations, but it is really difficult to try to outline realistic assumptions in which to recognize it as a phenomenon similar to the Internet, let alone think of it as its successor.

To date, the metaverse is made up of a series of interesting experiences to generate new business opportunities, but from here to revolutionize forever the way we communicate, it's a long way. So what will be the scenario that we can expect, at least in the near future?

Explaining why a single metaverse does not exist is much easier than trying to explain what it could be. There are many reasons why it is not feasible at the moment, starting from the immaturity of the enabling technologies, which limits the field of investigation to hypotheses and suggestions, with the impression that it will be like this for some time to come.

When we read the reports that inform us that in 2025 the metaverse business will be x or y billion dollars, we know very well that they refer to the path currently taken, consisting of many individual branded metaverses, those autonomous 3D virtual worlds where companies will find fertile ground to extend their businesses thanks to new digital experiences. To date, however, the conditions for interconnecting such a variety of metaverses appears somewhat nebulous.

In order to create the metaverse with a capital H, understood as the only multiverse capable of encompassing the multitude of individual metaverses, it would first be necessary to define a common consortium, as happened in 1994 with the W3C to manage the regulation of Internet services. A "super partes" authority, capable of defining standards, communication protocols and all aspects useful to guarantee the correct interoperability of the services themselves, allowing anyone to access the world wide web.

Whether we are talking about 2D web pages or 3D virtual worlds, it is essential the action of a body participated by the main public and private stakeholders, universally recognized, sufficiently representative and authoritative to be able to impose reference standards. The road in this sense still seems very long and nothing concrete has been established yet. It is said that the metaverse will be everyone's, but in the meantime everyone is racing to develop their own to seek a position of competitive advantage.

It should also be pointed out that, since the formation of the W3C, times have changed profoundly. Thirty years ago, it was in everyone's interest to create an environment that would allow the development of new businesses, and no one could have imagined that the Internet would lead us to where we are today, totally overturning social and economic models on a global level.

The pioneering momentum of the early days of the web has gradually given way to positions of dominance, where big tech has a strong position that sees them absolutely interested in creating new business platforms, without however risking losing the hegemony they enjoy. On the opposite front, governments are once again starting late, as technology always runs faster than the regulatory design.

Aware of the risks and opportunities that lie ahead, it will be necessary to find from the outset a fundamental condition of balance so that the metaverse becomes a real opportunity for development for everyone, as well as the real manifestation of the dystopian scenarios described so far in the sci-fi imagination.

Jeff H. Bolton
METAVERSE

Thank you for making it to the end of this book, we hope it was informative and able to provide you with all the tools you need to achieve your goals, whatever they may be.

This book has tried to highlight all the important points so that you can get all the benefits of this new digital revolution without having to deal with the negative effects.

All you need to do is to follow the information provided in the book and follow the directions.

I hope this book will really help you achieve your goals.

JEFF H. BOLTON
META
VERSE
THE NEW DIGITAL REVOLUTION. A
BEGINNER'S GUIDE TO INVESTING IN THE
DIGITAL ARTS OF THE FUTURE. NFT,
BLOCHCHAIN GAMING AND
CRYPTOCURRENCY

Jeff H. Bolton
METAVERSE